DRIVEN

Driven

A 107 YEAR FIGHT FOR EQUALITY

Simone Ray Thomas

Daryl Ramon Thomas &
Oluwaseyi G. Akintunde

Unheard Of Learning

Dedication

For Aniya Simone

Because you have always known the truth:

that you deserve to be free.

Contents

Acknowledgements

Thanks always to my "sun" Ramon, who is already the writer I hope to become. Your insights challenge me and make me better. They made this book better. Don't tell anybody I said it, but you are surely smarter than me.

Thank you also to Oluwaseyi for stepping up to help me when I needed it. Your suggestions gave me a fresh lens through which to see this work. Thank you for being the literary voice of reason that gave us the balance we needed.

You are both important to the world. Do big things!

Mr. Ernest Donelson II, thank you for your work and giving spirit.

I have immeasurable gratitude for my friends and family who continue to support me as I bring this vision to life. I know I am equal parts boring and obsessive. Thank you for putting up with me, for buying books, for telling other people about the books, for keeping me sane, and for just letting me be me.

Introduction

"Give me your tired, your poor, your huddled masses yearning to breathe free…" These words are carved on the Statue of Liberty, standing in New York Harbor as a symbol of America's promise of freedom for all. Our national anthem also tells us we're in "the land of the free." Since before America was even a country, millions of people have come here looking for a better life. And often they find just that.

But black Americans have a very different history. Most early black Americans did not come here in search of a better life. Instead, they were brought here by force. The first set of enslaved Africans arrived in America on August 20, 1619, over 400 years ago. For 246 years, few black Americans had any freedom or control over their own lives, bodies, or families. In much of America, **chattel slavery** lasted until June 19, 1865. Since that time, black people in this country have fought to fully enjoy the freedoms of American citizenship.

Even though the practice of enslaving black people came to an end in 1865, this did not mean that all Americans were ready to accept black people as their neighbors and equal citizens. Many still believed that black people- even those who had never been enslaved- were not as good as others. They wanted black people to stay in their place as second-class citizens. And some tried everything they could to keep them in that place. The fight to end **discrimination** has been a long and complicated one.

chattel slavery- a system in which the enslaved have no human rights

discrimination- unfair treatment of one or more groups

1

Separate

The War Between the States

Have you heard of the Civil War? It was fought from 1861-1865 between northern American states and southern American states. The war started, in part, because the southern states did not want to free the enslaved people. When the federal government tried to force them to do it, the southern states decided to separate from America and form their own country.

Public Domain Image

The Confederate States of America- Alabama, Florida, Georgia, Louisiana, Mississippi, South Carolina, and Texas- went to war to protect the right of states to make their own laws without the federal government getting in the way. The United States, or the Union, went to war to keep the country together. After four years of fighting, the Union won the war. The Confederate states rejoined the country and were forced to free all black Americans from slavery.

Rebuilding America

What came after the war was a period called Reconstruction. 'Construction' is just another word for 'building.' Between 1865-1877 America was trying to rebuild itself and trying to figure out just what to do with her newest citizens. During Reconstruction, black Americans were recognized as citizens for the first time and given the right to vote. For 12 years, soldiers were sent to the southern states to protect the newly freed people from violence because some folks refused to accept that they were no longer property and now had rights.

In 1877, Reconstruction ended and the soldiers left the south. **Segregation** quickly became a way of life.

The southern states all passed laws ensuring that black people and white people lived in separate neighborhoods, went to separate schools, and used separate restrooms and water fountains. Some restaurants didn't serve black people at all, and others made them pick up their orders from a door or window in the back of the building. Many public places either kept black people out or only admitted them on particular days. For example, many city zoos had "Negro

Day" on one day each week. All other days were for white visitors only.

Source: Library of Congress

A black person could not even walk into a department store and try on a pair of shoes. They had to draw an outline of their foot on a large piece of paper—usually an old grocery bag—and carry that into the store to choose the proper shoe size.

Segregation limited almost every aspect of black southerners' lives.

Almost 20 years after the end of Reconstruction, one case led the **U.S. Supreme Court** to make a decision about whether these laws were constitutional or not. And that was about public transportation. In the *Plessy v. Ferguson* case, the Supreme Court decided that "separate but equal" was legal in the United States. It was okay to have separate spaces for black and white people, as long as the black spaces were "equal" to the white spaces. The trouble was, most often the "separate" part of the law was enforced but not the "equal" part.

Public transportation was tricky. It would be too expensive to have separate trains and buses for black and white riders. So they found other ways to keep people apart. Usually, the seats in the front were for white riders, and the seats in the back were for black riders. A crowded train or bus meant that black riders had to give up their seats altogether. Often on city buses, black riders had to climb the front steps, pay the driver, get off, and then go to a back door to get back on. Sometimes drivers would leave them after they had already paid their fares.

For trains and buses that traveled across the country, "separate but equal" was even more complicated. A traveler going from a northern city to a southern city would face one set of laws in the north, and then another set of laws when they entered the south. It was possible that a black rider could ride in the front of a bus at the beginning of a trip, and then have to move to the back once they entered the segregated states.

Throughout history, black Americans spoke out against the system of "separate but equal" because it was never truly equal at all. They wanted to have the same rights and privileges as other Americans– not special treatment, just the same– including sitting wherever they wanted to sit on public transportation.

The Beginning of the End

Almost everyone has heard of Rosa Parks. In December 1955 she refused to move to the back of a segregated bus in Montgomery, Alabama. Her arrest sparked one of the most famous protests in American history, the Montgomery Bus Boycott, and brought an unknown young preacher named Martin Luther King, Jr. to the world's attention.

The story of Rosa Parks is actually one of the last chapters in a much longer story. By the time Mrs. Parks was arrested, black Americans had been fighting for equal treatment on public transportation for over 100 years. And even though the Montgomery Bus Boycott was successful in the end, the fight was still far from over.

the federal government- the government that controls the whole United States

segregation- the forced separation of different groups, in this case, on the basis of race

U.S. Supreme Court- the highest court in the country; a state supreme court is the highest in that state but not equal to the U.S. Supreme Court

Chapter 1 Discussion Questions

1. Why do you think some laws are made by the federal government instead of just letting each state decide for itself?

2. Why do you think black people couldn't try on shoes when they went shopping? If we asked a store owner at the time, what reasons might they offer?

3. Would you shop at a store that wouldn't let you try on anything? Why or why not?

4. What do you think the Supreme Court had in mind when they supported "separate but equal"? Is this idea really possible?

2

Early Battles: Coast to Coast

New York

Since the late 1700s, New York City has had more residents than any other city in America. When you think of transportation in New York City, you probably picture subway trains speeding through underground tunnels or hovering on rails high above the city. But in the 1850s many people in New York and other cities got around on something called a streetcar. Streetcars looked like small trolley trains, and horses pulled them along a track. They were owned by private companies and people had to buy tickets to ride them from one part of town to another. Some streetcars allowed black passengers to ride; others did not.

Public Domain Image

Slavery once existed in New York, but a law passed in 1799 brought it to an end. By the 1850s, New York had the largest free black population in the country. Many of these free people had money and owned property. Thomas Jennings was a well-known businessman in this community. He was a **tailor** and invented a process called dry scouring; this was the first method for dry cleaning clothes. Jennings was the first black person to be granted a **patent** by the US government. He owned his invention, and other people could not use it to make money without his permission.

Elizabeth Jennings
Public Domain Image

Elizabeth Jennings was Thomas Jennings' daughter. She was a teacher at one of New York's African Free Schools. The schools were created by wealthy white **abolitionists** in 1787 to educate black children. At first, they were supported by charity donations, but by the 1850s they were part of New York City's public school system.

On the morning of July 16, 1854, Elizabeth Jennings was running late. It was a Sunday and she was to play the organ for a church service. To save some time, she decided to take a streetcar operated by Third Avenue Railroad Company. Once the driver realized that she was a black woman, he asked her to get off the streetcar. Elizabeth

Jennings refused. The driver grabbed her and tried to force her off. But when he realized he couldn't do it by himself, he found a policeman to help.

Publisher Horace Greeley described Jennings's experience in New York's most popular newspaper, *The New York Tribune*:

> The conductor undertook to get her off, first alleging the car was full; when that was shown to be false, he pretended the other passengers were displeased at her presence; but (when) she insisted on her rights, he took hold of her by force to expel her. She resisted. The conductor got her down on the platform, jammed her bonnet, soiled her dress and injured her person. Quite a crowd gathered, but she **effectually** resisted. Finally, after the car had gone on further, with the aid of a policeman they succeeded in removing her.

The next day, New York's black community held a rally at the Jennings' church. They were tired of being mistreated on the streetcars. Even though some streetcars had signs that read "Colored Persons Allowed", black riders never knew what to expect. Even on a streetcar that allowed black passengers, they could be kicked off if another passenger complained about having to ride with them, or even if the conductor just felt like it. And Elizabeth Jennings being attacked by a conductor was just too much!

Thomas Jennings was connected to some of New York's most powerful people, black and white. He decided to sue the

Third Avenue Railway Company and hired a young lawyer named Chester A. Arthur to argue the case. Arthur was only 24 years old at the time, but he would later become the 21st President of the United States.

The case also caught the attention of famed black abolitionist Frederick Douglass. Douglass ran an abolitionist newspaper called the *North Star*. He wrote about what happened to Jennings and brought national attention to her case. A judge ruled in Elizabeth Jennings' favor in 1855. Third Avenue Railway Company had to pay her $250 as punishment, plus $22.50 to replace her torn clothes. As a result, and maybe to avoid future lawsuits, the company ended segregation on all of its streetcars.

The fight in New York wasn't over yet, though. There were three other streetcar companies that still practiced segregation. So did the stagecoaches, steamboats, and railroads. Black community leaders formed the New York Legal Rights Association to fight for equal treatment on all public transportation. For the next 10 years, the Association raised money to help people file lawsuits when they were faced with discrimination on any form of public transportation in New York.

In 1864, ten years after the Jennings case, a widow named Ellen Anderson sued a policeman who helped to remove her from a segregated streetcar. Many people sympathized with Mrs. Anderson because her husband was killed while fighting for the Union in the Civil War. Ellen Anderson won her lawsuit and in 1865– the same year that chattel slavery ended in the south– segregation was finally outlawed on all public transportation in New York.

California

While New Yorkers were fighting to end segregation on public transit, a young black woman on the other side of the country was having an experience very similar to Elizabeth Jennings. Charlotte Brown lived in San Francisco, California. She left her home on the evening of April 17, 1863, heading to a doctor's appointment. She walked a block and then boarded a streetcar. Like in New York, the streetcars in San Francisco were pulled by horses.

The conductor asked Charlotte to get off the streetcar and, like Elizabeth Jennings, she refused.

> The conductor went around and collected tickets and when he came to me I handed him my ticket and he refused to take it. It was one of the Omnibus Railroad tickets, one that I had purchased of them previous to that time. He replied that colored persons were not allowed to ride. I told him I had been in the habit of riding ever since the cars had been running. I answered that I had a great ways to go and I was later than I ought to be.

At first, the conductor didn't bother her. But when a white passenger started to complain about having to ride with a black person, the conductor grabbed her and pulled her off the car.

Charlotte's father hired a lawyer to sue Omnibus Railroad Company, the company that operated that streetcar. After over two years of fighting in court, Charlotte won her case, and the conductor was found guilty of assaulting her. The Omnibus Railroad Company had to pay Charlotte $500.

People in San Francisco's small black community understood that, even though the court decided in Charlotte's favor, it didn't mean that they would suddenly be welcome on all the streetcars. Just like in New York, black riders were treated differently depending on the conductor. A writer in San Francisco's black-owned *Pacific Appeal* newspaper joked about some white drivers being afraid to pick up black passengers.

> There are a certain number of the employees of this Company, who, if a colored person attempts to cross the street while their car is passing, are seized with a sudden fit of Negrophobia, which is generally manifested by pulling their alarm bell violently, as if some danger was **imminent**.

He went on to point out that some white passengers would be afraid to ride with even the most "respectable" black women.

The Omnibus Railroad Company argued that they were protecting white women and children by keeping black people off the streetcars. A cartoon in a local white newspaper showed white women riding on the streetcar surrounded by black people. The size of the black passengers was exaggerated to make it seem like they were crushing the tiny, helpless women.

Source: California Historical Society

When the judge ruled in favor of Charlotte Brown, some people accused him of being more worried about black people's convenience than he was about white people's safety. Others questioned whether Charlotte Brown was black at all because her skin was so light. Maybe she was a white woman who pretended to be black so she could make up a lawsuit and get money from the streetcar company.

A few years after Charlotte Brown won her case, a

well-known black abolitionist named Mary Ellen Pleasant also sued Omnibus Railroad Company for kicking her and two other black women off one of its streetcars. The women dropped their lawsuit after Omnibus made a promise to San Francisco's black citizens: from then on, they would be allowed to ride the streetcars without being bothered.

Pleasant then filed another lawsuit against another transit company, the North Beach & Mission Railroad company, claiming that they also discriminated against black passengers. This case made it all the way to the California Supreme Court in 1866. When the court decided in Pleasant's favor two years later, they permanently outlawed segregation on all public transportation in the state of California.

These women fought and won early battles in the fight against discrimination on public transportation in their states. But not every upcoming battle would be as successful.

tailor- a person who makes clothes especially to fit the wearer

patent- a license from the government, to keep others from selling a unique invention

abolitionists- activists who fought to end slavery

effectually- effectively

imminent- about to happen

patent- a license from the government, to keep others from selling a unique invention

abolitionists- activists who fought to end slavery

effectually- effectively

imminent- about to happen

Chapter 2 Discussion Questions

1. All northern states got rid of slavery by 1804. Why do you think the southern states held on to this system for so much longer?

2. Ellen Anderson gained a lot of support because her husband fought in the Civil War. Should the families of soldiers receive special treatment? Why or why not?

3. How were Elizabeth Jennings and Charlotte Brown's experiences similar? How were they different?

4. What do you think of the political cartoon? What was the artist trying to say?

5. Mary Ellen Pleasant was a well-known activist. Do you think this impacted how she was treated by the courts?

3

Homer Plessy & Jim Crow

America got its first railroad in 1827; it only traveled 13 miles. By 1852, the Boston and Ohio line connected the East coast to the Ohio River Valley. The first railroad to stretch across the country was completed in 1869. America was growing, and trains made it easier for people and products to travel from one side of the country to the other.

Cities replaced their old horse-drawn streetcars with electric ones, and some started using subway trains in the early 1900s. By the 1930s, buses were in common use across America. As public transportation grew, so did its problems.

During the early twentieth century, there were large protests in over 25 cities where blacks were either not allowed to ride public transportation or were mistreated when they did. People took to the streets, filed lawsuits, and staged **boycotts.** Most of the protests were unsuccessful or only had temporary success. In Richmond, Virginia, for example, black riders staged a boycott of the streetcars in 1904. Many white riders joined in, and they ultimately drove the company out of business. Unfortunately, this successful boycott did lead Virginia to end its segregation laws. In fact, Virginia made those laws even stricter in 1906.

And Virginia wasn't unique. Throughout the southern states, most public transit systems maintained some form of segregation. The phrase "separate but equal" came from a court case about black people riding on trains.

Homer Plessy

In 1890, the Louisiana **legislature** passed a law that required separate train cars for black riders. It was called the Separate Car Act. Many white people supported the law because it kept them from having to ride alongside black passengers. Black riders, however, saw the law as yet another attempt to take away the rights they had enjoyed during Reconstruction.

Unlike most previous cases, the railroad company was on the side of the black riders. It would cost them too much money to add more cars so that people could be kept apart. The state of Louisiana was cutting into its profits.

The Citizens Committee was a group of black community leaders from New Orleans. They worked with the railroad to develop a plan to prove that Louisiana's new law was **unconstitutional**. They decided to find a black person who was willing to break the law and get arrested. Then that person would go to court and defend themselves by claiming that the law was unconstitutional. They knew that they would probably lose the case in Louisiana, but then they could appeal to a federal court.

Homer Plessy was their man. He agreed to board an all-white car and be arrested on purpose. Plessy was mixed-race and very light-skinned. Some people thought he looked white, but the conductor on the train knew he was black. Remember, the railroad and the black people were on the same side. Following their plan, the driver called the police on Homer Plessy for breaking Louisiana law. When Plessy went on trial, his lawyers argued that the law requiring separate cars was a violation of his **14th Amendment** rights. As expected back then, he was convicted and the court charged him a $25 fine. That's the same as $765 now.

John H. Ferguson was the judge that found Homer Plessy guilty. When Plessy appealed to federal court, the case was called Plessy v. Ferguson because Homer Plessy was now fighting against the legal decision of Judge Ferguson.

Jim Crow

Plessy v. Ferguson became one of the most famous cases in history. The United States Supreme Court decided that judge Ferguson's decision in the state court was the correct decision. Louisiana's law was just fine, and they had the right to make the railroad follow that law when it operated in their state.

The Supreme Court was very specific in its ruling. They said it was legal to have separate cars for black passengers, as long as those cars were equal to the cars for white passengers. The highest court in the country was confirming that segregation– "separate but equal"– was legal according to the Constitution.

This decision gave the southern states the Court's permission to keep their segregation laws and to make new ones. They came to be called "Jim Crow" laws. Jim Crow was a fictional character made up by a white actor, to make fun of black people. The character was enslaved but very lazy. The actor, Thomas Rice, painted his skin black– not dark brown, like real skin, but actually black– and he sang and danced and played mean tricks on people.

The Jim Crow character became a symbol representing the belief that black people were stupid, lazy, dangerous, and dishonest. "Jim Crow laws" were largely based on these racist beliefs.

The *Plessy vs. Ferguson* decision made it clear that the Supreme Court saw segregation as constitutional. Still, it left some other important questions unanswered. When Homer Plessy got arrested, the train was traveling

Public Domain Image

from New Orleans, Louisiana to Covington, Louisiana. No other states were involved. The court's decision only applied to transportation in an already-segregated state. So what was supposed to happen when a train or bus traveled from one state to another? It would take many more years and many more arrests to answer that question.

boycotts- a large group of people refusing to buy or use something

legislature- the group of people who make laws in a state or country

unconstitutional- against the Constitution or different than the Constitution

14th Amendment- added to the Constitution in 1868, it says that all citizens have equal rights

Chapter 3 Discussion Questions

1. Why do you think protests sometimes led to stricter laws?

2. Homer Plessy got arrested on purpose to challenge the law in Louisiana. Was he foolish or brave? Explain your response.

3. The Jim Crow character was created to make fun of black people. Can you think of other fictional characters that make fun of a person or group?

4

Across State Lines

*It's 1942. A black man climbs onto a bus in Louisville, Kentucky, heading to Nashville, Tennessee. He is tall and thin, wearing a suit and tie, and has a small afro. He's a handsome man, with skin the color of honey, and a neat mustache. As the man enters the bus, a playful toddler reaches for his tie. The toddler's mother screams, "Don't touch him. You never play with a n*gger!" She pulls her child away. At that moment, the man decides to show the toddler that, despite what the mother said, he is not a "n*gger."*

He's a man, and no man wants to be treated like he's less than human, so he sits down in the second row of seats. It's illegal for him to sit there, in the front. Kentucky is a Jim Crow state and black passengers are supposed to ride in the back. He knows he will be arrested. But he sits down anyway because he wants this young child to see that not all black people willingly accept segregation.

Bayard Rustin spent his entire adult life fighting against

injustice. He would later become one of the original "freedom riders", a labor organizer, an advisor to Martin Luther King, and the driving force behind the 1963 March on Washington for Jobs and Freedom. He was involved in important social justice movements from the 1940s to the 1980s. But that day in 1942, he was just a black man breaking the law.

The driver asked him to move to the back of the bus. He didn't. Some other drivers came onto the bus and unsuccessfully tried to convince him. The bus eventually left Kentucky with Rustin still sitting in the second row. The ride took about four hours. Just outside Nashville, police stopped the bus. They took Rustin off, beaten him up, then hauled him off to the police station. They let him go after a few hours, and no charges were ever filed against Rustin or against the officers that beat him.

Just a few years later, the fight to end segregation on interstate buses would make it all the way to the Supreme Court. And Bayard Rustin would break the same law again, and end up in prison on a **chain gang**.

Public Domain Image

Elmer Henderson, 1942

Even the most wealthy and influential black people were subject to discrimination in interstate travel. Elmer Henderson worked for the United States government and traveled for his job. In 1942 he took a Southern Railways train from Washington D.C. to Atlanta, Georgia. He was riding first class.

Passenger trains have kitchens and dining cars where passengers eat during scheduled meal times. In the dining car on Southern Railways, the tables closest to the kitchen were usually set aside for black passengers. A curtain was used to keep them separate from the white passengers.

When Elmer Henderson entered the dining car to have his dinner, there were white passengers seated at the black table. This was normal when there were no black passengers present. But Elmer Henderson was present. And he wasn't allowed to sit anywhere else. The **steward** refused to ask the folks to move, or to allow Mr. Henderson to sit at one of the other tables alongside white passengers. Instead, he told Elmer Henderson to wait, that he could eat at the designated black table when the others were finished with their meal.

Mr. Henderson did as he was told. He left the dining car and waited for the steward to come and get him once his table was available. The steward never came. The dinner service ended and the dining car was closed without Mr. Henderson being served.

The 14th Amendment to the Constitution says that all Americans have equal legal rights and that you cannot discriminate against a person because of their skin color. Mr. Henderson filed a complaint with the **Interstate Commerce Commission (ICC)**. This government agency controls businesses that operate in more than one state. They decided that the railroad had violated Mr. Henderson's rights because he did not get the same service as the white first-class passengers. They ordered the railroad to get rid of the separate tables for black passengers and the curtain. This decision effectively ended segregation in railroad dining cars.

Two years later a young woman without any of Henderson's wealth and influence would strike another, even bigger, blow to segregation in interstate travel.

Irene Morgan, 1944

Irene Morgan was a 27-year-old wife and mother from Baltimore, Maryland. Baltimore is about 40 miles away from the nation's capital, Washington D.C. In the 1940s, about 20% of the people who lived in Baltimore were black. Many of them migrated there from the

Irene Morgan
Source: The Afro American (Newspaper), June 15, 1946

south to work in factories. Because Baltimore is so close to Washington D.C., many of its factories made equipment for American forces fighting in World War II. Mrs. Morgan worked in a factory that made parts for B-26 Marauder fighter planes.

After suffering a serious medical condition in the Spring of 1944, Mrs. Morgan traveled south to Virginia to recover at her mother's house. On July 16, she headed back to Baltimore to return to work. There were no signs marking a black section or a white section on the bus, but there were rules. A black passenger could not sit in the same row as a white passenger, even if that was the only available seat.

Irene boarded the bus and took a seat next to a young black woman who was holding her baby. About 30 miles into the trip, the bus stopped in Middlesex County, Virginia to pick up more passengers. A white couple got onto the bus and wanted to sit where Irene and the other young mother were sitting. The bus driver told them to get up and move. Irene repeatedly said 'no', and tried to get the other woman to refuse, as well. Even though she wasn't doing anything wrong, the young mother didn't want to make trouble; she got up and moved to the back of the bus with her baby. Irene stayed seated.

The bus driver drove to the nearest jail and went inside to find a sheriff. The sheriff came onto the bus and handed Irene an arrest warrant. The bus driver claimed that she was in the "white section" of the bus, even though there was no clear dividing line. According to him, she was breaking Virginia law. Irene took the warrant from the officer, tore it up, and flung it out the open window.

The sheriff tried to grab her and make her get up. She kicked him in his private parts. Mrs. Morgan later described the ordeal:

He touched me. That's when I kicked him in a very bad place. He hobbled off and another one came on. I was going to bite him, but he looked dirty, so I clawed him instead. I ripped his shirt. We were both pulling at each other. He said he would use his nightstick. I said, "We'll whip each other."

The second officer got away from Irene and got off the bus to get a deputy to help him. Together, they managed to drag her off the bus. Irene was taken to jail and charged with resisting arrest and with refusing to obey Virginia's segregation laws.

When she went to court three months later, Irene Morgan admitted to resisting arrest and agreed to pay a fine of $100. But she wouldn't admit to breaking the segregation laws because she felt the laws were wrong. The National Association for the Advancement of Colored People (NAACP) stepped in to help her. The NAACP was and still is the largest civil rights organization in the country. It was founded in 1910 "to eliminate race-based discrimination." They have a legal fund that pays for lawyers for people who are fighting important legal cases.

Mrs. Morgan appealed her case to the Virginia Supreme Court, the highest court in the state. That court said she was guilty. But Mrs. Morgan and her NAACP lawyer, Thurgood Marshall, maintained that the Virginia Law did not apply to her because she was a resident of Maryland, where segregation on buses did not exist. They decided to sue the state of Virginia, and the case went to the United States Supreme

Court. Many years later, the lawyer Thurgood Marshall would become the first black Supreme Court Justice.

No state can pass laws that violate citizens' 14th Amendment rights. People expected Irene Morgan and the NAACP to argue that the state of Virginia had passed such a law.

Mrs. Morgan's legal team decided to take a different approach. There is a part of the Constitution that says that one state cannot make laws that have a negative effect on businesses in other states. This is called the Commerce Clause. So, if a business operates in many states, like an interstate bus company, one state cannot pass laws that could cause that business to lose money in other states.

The Supreme Court sided with Irene Morgan, Thurgood Marshall, and the NAACP. They decided that segregation on interstate buses was a violation of the Commerce Clause, because travelers may not spend money on bus tickets if they knew that they would have to deal with Jim Crow laws once they reached the south. In this case, segregation laws in Virginia could cause the bus company to lose money in Maryland. So, in June 1946, the Court ruled that any segregation on buses traveling from state to state was unconstitutional.

The Journey of Reconciliation, 1947

The whole country is supposed to follow Supreme Court decisions. Still, the southern states held on to their segregation laws and continued to enforce them on trains and interstate buses.

A group called CORE, the Congress of Racial Equality, set

out to prove that the two largest bus companies, Greyhound and Trailways, were still segregating passengers in the south. Bayard Rustin was one of its founders. CORE was made up of both black and white activists who believed in using non-violent methods to challenge racism. They decided to do a test. Sixteen activists– eight black and eight white- would ride through the "upper south" for two weeks to see what happened when they didn't follow local Jim Crow laws. They called it the Journey of Reconciliation.

CORE knew that it was far too dangerous to take such an action in the "deep south". South Carolina, Georgia, Alabama, Florida, Louisiana, and Mississippi were known for violence against black people, especially those trying to upset their way of life. Virginia, North Carolina, Tennessee, and Kentucky were believed to be safer. Still, The NAACP and other civil rights organizations discouraged the Journey of Reconciliation. They thought it was still too dangerous, and it might not do much good.

Source: Library of Congress

On April 9, 1947, the sixteen men boarded buses in Washington D.C., half of them riding Greyhound and the other half riding Trailways. They had no problems in Washington D.C. or Virginia. Sometimes the black and white riders sat side by side. Sometimes black CORE riders sat in the front, while the white riders sat in the back.

By April 11, just two days into the journey, trouble started brewing. Passing through Oxford, North Carolina the bus driver asked Bayard Rustin to move to a seat in the back. Rustin refused to move, the police refused to arrest him, and the driver refused to drive the bus with a black man sitting in the front. All of this stubbornness caused a 45-minute delay, but the bus eventually reached its destination.

Two days later, in Chapel Hill, North Carolina four CORE riders were arrested, two black and two white. The black men had refused to move to the back of the bus, and the two white men had interfered with their arrest. When another white CORE rider tried to go to the police station and post **bond** for those arrested, he was violently attacked by local taxi drivers. Still, the Journey continued. All 16 riders made it safely back to Washington, D.C.

A month after the arrests in Chapel Hill, the four returned to North Carolina for their trial. The judge found them all guilty. The black men, one of them Bayard Rustin, were sentenced to 30 days of hard labor on a chain gang in a North Carolina prison. The two white men were sentenced to 90 days each. The judge wanted to send a strong warning to white Americans: there would be harsh punishments for trying to help black people end segregation.

The Journey of Reconciliation highlighted the southern states' refusal to obey the Supreme Court, and little was done to make them obey. But the Journey also showed the power of **direct action** protests. The riders had purposely broken local laws so that they could put injustice on display. This became the model for many protests during the Civil Rights

Movement of the 1950s and 60s, including the explosive 1961 Freedom Rides.

Sarah Keys, 1952

Sarah Keys
Public Domain Image

Sarah Keys was a private in the Women's Army Corps, a branch of the United States Army. She was **stationed** at the Fort Dix Army base in New Jersey and caught a Carolina Coach bus home to Washington D.C. to spend time with her family. In the middle of the night, her bus made a stop in the small town of Roanoke Rapids, North Carolina.

A new bus driver took over. The driver began checking every passenger's ticket. When he got to Private Keys, he didn't check hers. Instead, he told her to move to a seat further back because a white marine wanted her seat. She refused, stating simply that she was comfortable where she was. The driver moved on to the next passenger and went on checking tickets.

Soon the driver announced that they would be switching buses. When Private Keys attempted to leave with the others, he told her to stay where she was, since she was so comfortable there. She would not be getting on the other bus. Shortly after, policemen arrived and arrested Private Keys for failing to move when the driver asked her to. Private Keys was taken to jail and placed in a cell until the next afternoon. She was not allowed to call her family.

The local court found Sarah Keys guilty and sentenced her to pay a fine of $25. But Sarah Keys refused to accept that verdict. She and her father reached out to the NAACP for help. The NAACP paired her with a young black woman who'd recently graduated from Howard University Law School, Dovey Johnson Roundtree. Attorney Roundtree took Sarah Keys' case very personally. Before becoming a lawyer, Roundtree had also been a member of the Women's Army Corps. And she had her own experience of race-based harassment on an interstate bus.

Their first legal strategy was to appeal to the U.S. District Court in Washington D.C. The court refused to rule on the case, saying that it was not in their **jurisdiction**. Keys and her attorney decided to make an appeal to the Interstate Commerce Commission. The Commission took its time in reaching a decision.

Eight months later, in May 1954, the U.S. Supreme Court decided that "separate but equal" didn't work in public schools. In its historic *Brown v. Board of Education* decision, the court made segregation illegal in schools. The Interstate Commerce Commission followed their lead and sided with Sarah Keys in her dispute with the bus company. The commission ruled that segregation on buses or in bus terminals was unconstitutional. The decision was released to the public in November 1955, just one week before the arrest of Mrs. Rosa Parks in Montgomery, Alabama.

chain gang- a group of prisoners chained together while working

steward- a person who takes care of the passengers on a train, ship, or airplane

Commerce - business

bond-a payment made to get people out of jail before they go on trial

direct action- a type of protest that involves doing something physical instead of negotiating or filing a complaint or lawsuit

stationed- assigned to work

jurisdiction- the power to make legal decisions

Chapter 4 Discussion Questions

1. Bayard Rustin got arrested the first time trying to prove a point to a toddler. Do you think a small child could understand his actions?

2. Think about the steward in the Elmer Henderson case. What could he have done differently? Was there a solution that could have avoided the lawsuit and kept the steward out of trouble?

3. A judge gave the white CORE members a harsher sentence than the black CORE members. Do you think this would keep some white people from getting involved?

4. List some other direct action protests you have learned about in American history.

5

The Fight in Montgomery

Few blacks had cars in those days. We relied on the buses. It seemed that the white operators of the buses went out of their way to humiliate black passengers, despite the fact that the bus company derived the majority of its income from black riders.
–Attorney Fred Gray, *Bus Ride to Justice*

Alabama law legalized segregation on public transportation in 1900. This was yet another way to remove the freedoms black people briefly enjoyed during Reconstruction. Black passengers could not even walk through the front of the bus. They had to pay their fare, get off, and then come back on through a door in the back. The first four rows of seats were reserved for white riders. The middle section, often called "no man's land", was open to black passengers, but they had to move if the white section filled up. If a bus was very crowded, white passengers would take the seats in the back, too.

All of the drivers were white, and they were the authority on the buses. They didn't hesitate to remove any black rider who broke the rules or didn't follow their orders. Still, there were always black passengers who resisted.

Lillie Mae Bradford, 1951

Long before 1955, Black folks in Montgomery pushed back against the way bus drivers treated them. And the segregated seats weren't the only problem. In 1951, Lillie Mae Bradford was arrested for standing up to a driver who tried to cheat her out of money.

When you ride the bus, sometimes you have to take more than one to get to where you're going. When this happens, you pay extra for what they call a "transfer". Ms. Bradford did that on May 11, 1951, on her way home from her job working with disabled children. The driver punched her bus ticket but didn't give her credit for the transfer. She had to speak up, or she would have to pay again when she got to the second bus.

I thought if I don't get up and start speaking for my rights, I never will. It was humiliating. It was not dignified. It was off-limits to go up to the front of the bus but I went up there and I told him that my ticket hadn't been punched right. He said: 'N*gger, go to the back of the bus' and I said: 'I will, as soon as you give me the right transfer or give me my money back.' And then I took a seat in the white folks' section.

The driver refused to correct his mistake. So Lillie May Bradford stayed in the front seat. She was arrested for Disorderly Conduct and released after paying a fine. But the arrest affected her for the rest of her life. Now she had a criminal record and this always kept her from getting the jobs she really wanted.

1955

Claudette Colvin

Nine months before Rosa Parks was arrested, a fifteen-year-old girl named Claudette Colvin was arrested in Montgomery for refusing to give up her seat to a white passenger. Claudette was not an activist, but she was learning about **civil disobedience** from one of her teachers. She was fed up with Jim Crow laws and with her community being treated unfairly.

Black students in Montgomery could only attend two high schools, Booker T. Washington and George Washington Carver. Claudette went to "Booker Washington" and was devastated by what she saw happening to an older schoolmate named Jeremiah Reeves. Claudette witnessed Jeremiah's arrest for assaulting a white woman. According to Jeremiah, the police tortured him and made him confess. His trial lasted just two days, and an all-white jury found him guilty. The judge sentenced him to death. Montgomery's black community was outraged.

On March 2, 1955, Claudette and three of her friends were riding the bus home from school. They sat just behind "no man's land" in the front row of the black section. The white section filled up, and a white woman came and stood in the middle of their row. Claudette's friends got up and moved further back. Even though there were now three empty seats, the woman still wouldn't sit in the same row with Claudette. The driver told Claudette to move further back. She wouldn't.

The driver drove the bus to the central hub at Court Square downtown. When they arrived, the driver called for help from one of the **transit police**. The officer got on the bus and tried to talk Claudette into moving. When she wouldn't, he admitted that he did not have the authority to arrest her and left the bus.

The bus left Court Square and drove one block, where a city police car was waiting. Two officers came on and tried to get Claudette to either move back or get off. When she refused, they grabbed her arms and forced her off. Annie

Larkins, one of Claudette's friends on the bus that day, recalled Claudette yelling, "It's my constitutional right!" as she was dragged away.

The officers wrote in their police report: "We then informed Claudette that she was under arrest. She struggled off the bus and all the way to the police car." The officers claimed that Claudette hit them, but both she and her classmates denied this. Claudette was taken to the city jail where adults were held. They later released her to her mother and her pastor.

Claudette's community was proud of her, but they were also afraid. Fighting segregation brought the possibility of violence. The Ku Klux Klan was known to harass and even murder black people who took a stand. Her parents and neighbors kept watch throughout the night. Claudette later recalled her neighborhood's reaction, "Dad sat up all night with his shotgun...Probably nobody on King Hill slept that night."

The family called on E.D. Nixon for help. Mr. Nixon had been an organizer for the **Pullman porters union** and was known as an influential man in Montgomery's black community. Ten years earlier, in 1944, he had helped a woman named Viola White. Mrs. White had also been arrested for breaking segregation rules on a Montgomery bus. She was beaten by police and ordered to pay a fine. When she tried to appeal the fine, a policeman tried to scare her by kidnapping and assaulting her teenage daughter. E.D. Nixon had gotten a judge to put out a warrant for that policeman's arrest. Even though the officer left town before he could be arrested, very few black men had the power to do what Nixon had done. It was rare for any white person, especially a police officer, to be arrested for hurting a black person.

Mr. Nixon took three important steps to help Claudette. First, he talked a young lawyer named Fred Gray into taking Claudette's case. Next, he organized a meeting between the police, the bus company, and a group of leaders from the black community. This meeting was Martin Luther King Jr's first political action in Montgomery. Finally, Mr. Nixon connected Claudette to Mrs. Rosa Parks. Mrs. Parks was the youth leader and secretary of the Montgomery chapter of the NAACP. She got Claudette involved with the youth group and helped to raise money for her defense.

Claudette was charged with violating segregation laws, disturbing the peace, and assault. Annie Larkins testified for Claudette when she went to court. "There was no assault." Claudette hadn't hurt anyone or even tried to.

The judge found Claudette guilty and sentenced her to probation. When you're on probation, you have to follow certain rules and check in with a court-appointed officer, but you don't have to go to jail. He later dropped all the charges except for the assault. He didn't do this to help Claudette, though. If she wasn't charged with breaking the segregation laws, Fred Gray couldn't appeal and get a higher court to question those laws. The judge was protecting segregation from being overturned by the federal court if the case made it that far.

The black community was upset over the court's decision in Claudette's case. There was talk about boycotting the city buses. The Women's Political Council—a group that fought for the rights and protection of black women —had been meeting with city leaders to try to address the problems, but nothing had improved. Black women rode the buses more than any other group, but they had few rights and nowhere to turn when drivers mistreated them. The Council also got women more involved in the community, helped people register to vote, and supported women who were victims of violent crimes.

Black riders in Baton Rouge, Louisiana had successfully boycotted their city's bus system for six days in 1953. The buses there were still segregated, but the boycott made the rules clear, and black passengers no longer had to give up their seats to white passengers.

Montgomery wanted to bring about some change, too. They needed a spokesperson, someone to be the public face of a fight against the bus system. Leaders in the black community said that Claudette Colvin was too young for this role, and they questioned her emotional stability.

In a 1998 interview with the *Washington Post,* Ms. Colvin offered her own explanation for being pushed to the background of the very fight she'd started. "They didn't want me because I didn't represent the middle class... didn't want me involved because of where I lived and what my parents' background was." Claudette's family was poor. Her parents weren't educated, and they didn't belong to any of Montgomery's black organizations. They didn't socialize or go to church with any of Montgomery's black **elite**. In an interview with *The Guardian* in 2000, Ms. Colvin pointed out how some black people looked at communities like hers.

> Middle-class blacks looked down on King Hill...We had unpaved streets and outside toilets. We used to have a lot of **juke joints** up there, and maybe men would drink too much and get into a fight. It wasn't a bad area, but it had a reputation.

So Claudette Colvin was pushed to the background. Leaders doubted that black people in Montgomery would support her. They understood that staying off the buses would require sacrifice and that they had to get people riled up enough to do it.

Aurelia Browder

Just six weeks after Claudette Colvin's arrest, another black woman was arrested for refusing to move to the back of a city bus. Aurelia Browder was a widow and mother of six who worked hard to take care of her large family. She'd dropped out of high school as a teenager but went back to earn her diploma when she was in her early 30s.

At age 36, Mrs. Browder was a student at Alabama State College (now Alabama State University). There she met an English professor named Jo Ann Robinson. Robinson was president of the Women's Political Council. She and Aurelia Browder worked together on efforts to register more black voters.

Alabama required a **literacy test** in order to become a registered voter. In addition to going to college and raising her kids, Mrs. Browder was a volunteer tutor for people improving their reading skills. She also drove people to the polls, helped them to get registered, and spoke out against poll taxes. A poll tax was a fee that registered voters had to pay in order to cast their ballots. A lot of black people couldn't afford to pay, and this kept them away from the polls.

On April 19, 1955 Mrs. Browder sat in the white section of a city bus and ignored the driver's demands that she move. He called for the police to arrest her, and she was found guilty, of course. The judge ordered her to pay a fine.

Aurelia Browder's arrest didn't get a lot of attention at first. When the Montgomery Bus Boycott started months later, she used her car to help get people around. In addition to her work with the Women's Political Council, Mrs. Browder became a member of the Montgomery Improvement Association, the organization that planned and **facilitated** the boycott.

The following year Mrs. Browder became the lead **plaintiff** in the court battle that led to real change, *Browder v. Gayle*. As the lead plaintiff, her name was on the case even though there were four other plaintiffs. The defendant was William Gayle who was the mayor of Montgomery at the time. Attorney Fred Gray later explained why he chose Mrs. Browder as the lead plaintiff. "I chose her because she was a matured person, and I thought she would make an excellent first witness if I needed to put someone on [the stand]." Attorney Gray had faith that, if the time came, Mrs. Browder could speak for her fellow plaintiffs and for all of black Montgomery.

Mary Louise Smith & Suzie McDonald

On October 21, 1955, Mary Louise Smith rode a Montgomery bus to the home of a woman who owed her money. The previous week she'd worked as the woman's maid; her pay was supposed to be $2 per day. She'd worked Monday through Friday and half the day Saturday, but she wasn't paid at the end of the week. The woman owed her $11.

Mary Louise was careful to arrive early in the morning when she knew the woman would still be home. But no one answered the door. Mary Louise was angry and frustrated. Because she was black and the woman who owed her was white, she couldn't go to the police or other law enforcement for help. She went back to the bus to head home empty-handed.

Years later, Ms. Smith described her ordeal in a news article,

> I was sitting behind the sign that said 'For Colored.' A white lady got on the bus and she asked the bus driver to tell me to move out of my seat for her to sit there. He asked me to move three times, and I refused. So, he got up and said he would call the cops.

The police came and Smith was arrested and ordered to pay a $9 fine.

Like Claudette Colvin, leaders did not consider Mary Louise Smith an acceptable symbol to get blacks in Montgomery to boycott the buses. She was only 18 and someone started a rumor that her father was an alcoholic. Community leaders thought people might not have sympathy for Ms. Smith, at least not enough sympathy to walk to work.

Mary Louise Smith was never even aware that community leaders discussed using her case to spark a boycott. When she found out years later, she didn't care about not becoming famous like Rosa Parks. She was more concerned with the rumors about her father. According to both Smith and her sister, their father was a family man who worked a full-time job at a printing press and did odd jobs on weekends to support his children. He didn't even allow liquor in his house.

On the same day of Ms. Smith's arrest, an older woman named Susie McDonald was arrested, too. Black people in Montgomery knew "Miss Sue" and they knew she was black. Her skin and eyes were so light that white people couldn't always tell. But when they got confused, Miss Sue was quick to tell them she was a black woman. A widow, she received her husband's **pension** from the railroad and her family owned a place called McDonald's Farm, where black families went swimming and had picnics in the summer. This was a big deal in the 1950s when blacks were not allowed to swim in public pools or have family gatherings in public parks.

Very little is known about what really happened when Miss Sue was arrested, except that she was fined for breaking segregation laws and she was one of the plaintiffs in the *Browder v. Gayle* case. Some say she told the driver that she was black, and then sat down in the white section. Its almost certain that Miss Sue got arrested on purpose, though, much like Mrs. Rosa Parks less than six weeks later.

Rosa Parks, The Activist

Mrs. Rosa Parks spent many years dedicated to causes supporting the rights of black people and women. In 1943, she began going to NAACP meetings with her husband Raymond, who had been an active member for many years. They asked her to become their secretary because she was the only woman at the meetings.

Throughout the 1940s, Mrs. Parks also worked with her husband in the League of Women Voters, helping black people in and around Montgomery register to vote. She successfully registered to vote in 1945, after being rejected two times before that.

In 1944, on behalf of the NAACP, she went to investigate the violent attack of a black woman named Recy Taylor in Abbeville, Alabama. When local law enforcement failed to punish the men who attacked Ms. Taylor, Rosa Parks and other leaders created the Committee for Equal Justice for Mrs. Recey Taylor to bring national attention to the Taylor case. The committee established chapters all over the country —New York, Detroit, Chicago, and Denver—and fought to end violence against black women. The Committee for Equal Justice was celebrated as the largest national push for justice that America had seen in a long time.

In 1949, Mrs. Parks fought a similar fight for a Montgomery woman named Gertrude Perkins. Ms. Perkins had been attacked by two Montgomery police officers on her way home from a bus stop. When she reported it, the police department refused to arrest its own officers or to release their names. Mrs. Parks helped to form the Citizens Committee for Gertrude Perkins. The Committee, along with Ms. Perkins' church, led protests that eventually ran the guilty officers out of town.

By 1955 Rosa Parks had been the secretary of the Montgomery NAACP for eleven years. She was also the youth coordinator. In August—following the arrests of Claudette Colvin and Aurelia Browder, but before her own arrest—Mrs. Rosa Parks was sent to training at the Highlander Folk School in East Tennessee. Activists went to Highlander to learn leadership skills and strategies for **passive resistance**.

That same month, fourteen-year-old Emmett Till was beaten and murdered in Money, Mississippi. He was from Chicago, visiting relatives down south for the summer. A white woman named Carolyn Bryant accused him of flirting with her. Till was taken from his family's home, badly beaten, and killed.

The men charged with Till's murder were found not guilty by an all-white jury. Six months later they confessed during a magazine interview. Carolyn Bryant, the woman who accused Till of flirting, also later confessed that she had been lying about the young man. Emmitt Till's mother allowed Jet magazine, one of the most popular black magazines in America at the time, to publish photos of his body.

The pictures of the badly beaten boy sent waves of shock and sadness through the country. They gave many black southerners the motivation they needed to fight back. Rosa

Parks saw those pictures and Till was on her mind as she sat on the bus waiting to be arrested: "I thought of Emmett Till and I just couldn't go back." She'd had lunch with Attorney Fred Gray just a few hours earlier. The two worked less than two blocks apart and often spent lunchtimes discussing the fight for desegregation.

Mrs. Parks was arrested on the Cleveland Avenue bus just blocks from the spot where Claudette Colvin had been arrested nine months earlier. Her husband and Attorney Gray swiftly bailed her out.

This was the moment Jo Ann Robinson and other community leaders had been waiting for. In her memoir, Robinson recalled,

> The idea had been entertained for years. Almost daily some black man, woman, or child had had an unpleasant experience on the bus and told other members of the family about it at the supper table or around the open fireplace or stove.

Now leaders had the case that black Montgomery would get behind. That same evening, Jo Ann Robinson and the Women's Political Council started passing out flyers in Montgomery's black communities:

Another woman has been arrested and thrown in jail because she refused to get up out of her seat on the bus for a white person to sit down. It is the second time since the Claudette Colvin case that a Negro woman has been arrested for the same thing. This has to be stopped. Negroes have rights too, for if Negroes did not ride the buses, they could not operate. Three-fourths of the riders are Negro, yet we are arrested, or have to stand over empty seats. If we do not do something to stop these arrests, they will continue. The next time it may be you, or your daughter, or mother. This woman's case will come up on Monday. We are, therefore, asking every Negro to stay off the buses Monday in protest of the arrest and trial. Don't ride the buses to work, to town, to school, or anywhere on Monday. You can afford to stay out of school for one day if you have no other way to go except by bus. You can also afford to stay out of town for one day. If you work, take a cab, or walk. But please, children and grown-ups, don't ride the bus at all on Monday. Please stay off all buses Monday.

For years, young people have been taught that Mrs. Parks refused to move because she was tired. In her own autobiography, Parks clearly says this isn't true.

> People always say that I didn't give up my seat because I was tired, but that isn't true. I wasn't tired physically, or no more tired than I usually was at the end of a working day. I was not old, although some people have an image of me being old then. I was forty-two. No, the only tired I was, was tired of giving in.

Mrs. Parks was arrested on a Thursday evening. On Friday, community leaders had a meeting to decide on a list of demands for the bus company. They weren't asking for any special treatment. They wanted the bus drivers to be respectful. They wanted seats to be first-come, first-served, with no segregated sections. They wanted the company to start hiring black drivers. The boycott would start on Monday. Black Montgomery residents were asked to stay off the buses until these demands were met.

By Saturday, December 3rd, it was clear that people were reading the flyers and agreed with the boycott. They were already staying off of the buses. On Sunday, black churches all over the city made announcements and advertised the boycott. On Monday, black people walked to school and work, hitchhiked, rode bikes, turned their everyday cars into taxis, and made **carpools**.

The Montgomery Bus Boycott was officially started. On Monday night, Dexter Avenue Baptist's new pastor, Martin Luther King Jr, gave a speech at Holt Street Baptist Church. He encouraged the black citizens of Montgomery to keep the boycott going.

News of the Montgomery Bus Boycott soon spread across the country. Black churches all over the United States started raising money to help the boycotters. Some collected shoes and sent them to Montgomery to help those who were walking long distances every day.

Two months after the boycott started, community leaders set out to prove that bus segregation was illegal. Rosa Parks couldn't be a part of this legal battle because she was still fighting her criminal case. Instead, Fred Gray represented the women who had been arrested before Parks: Aurelia Browder, Claudette Colvin, Susie McDonald, and Mary Louise Smith. They sued the city of Montgomery for discrimination.

In June of 1956, a **district court** ruled in the women's favor. They decided segregated buses were a violation of the 14th Amendment because black riders didn't get equal treatment. The city of Montgomery and the state of Alabama disagreed with the decision and appealed to the U.S. Supreme Court, but the Supreme Court agreed with the lower court's decision. In December 1956, the Supreme Court refused to deal with the case any further and ordered the city to desegregate the buses. The court sent federal police officers to hand-deliver the ruling to Mayor Gayle.

Attorney Fred Gray gave credit to Claudette Colvin for sparking the flames of change in Montgomery. "If there had been no Claudette Colvin, there may never have developed a Mrs. Rosa Parks as we know her, and there may never have developed a Dr. King." Claudette Colvin's story was captured in the 2009 biography *Twice Toward Justice*. In December 2021, 66 years after her arrest, she was finally able to have her juvenile criminal record removed.

The Montgomery Bus Boycott is often viewed as the first major victory in the Civil Rights Movement, but the fight to end racial discrimination on public transportation did not end there. The question was settled for local buses. But interstate travel was still a problem. Segregation on interstate buses had been illegal since Irene Morgan's case in 1944. But that didn't stop it from happening.

civil disobedience- breaking a law as a form of protest

transit police- police units that safeguard buses, trains, boats, and airplanes

Pullman porter's union- the first black workers union to successfully negotiate for their rights; They served train passengers.

elite- high class, special, better than the norm

juke joint- an informal nightclub, often in a large shack or a barn

literacy test- a test used to keep black people from voting, they often contained ridiculous questions

facilitate- to make something easier, often through careful planning

plaintiff- the person who files a lawsuit, or brings a legal complaint

pension- retirement money

passive resistance- nonviolent refusal to obey a law

carpools- ride-sharing with friends or associates

district court- a court run by the U.S. government, but not as powerful as the U.S. Supreme Court

Chapter 5 Discussion Questions

1. Even though people knew they would be arrested, they still broke segregation laws. Why do you think they did this?

2. In your own words, explain why Claudette Colvin's case wasn't used to spark the Montgomery Bus Boycott. Do you agree or disagree with this decision?

3. Why do people focus more on the Montgomery Bus Boycott than the *Browder v. Gayle* case, even though the case ended bus segregation?

A NOTE ABOUT JULIETTE HAMPTON MORGAN

Juliette Hampton Morgan had all the markings of high society: money, education, and connections to the "right" people. But she never drove because of her severe anxiety. She rode the bus to her job at the Montgomery Public Library. She saw how the drivers treated black riders. And she didn't like it.

When drivers would attempt to speed off as a black rider walked to the back

Source: Alabama Department of Archives and History

door- after that rider had already paid- Morgan would pull the emergency alarm to make the bus stop, and then scream at the driver until he let the rider on the bus. She also wrote letters to the local newspaper, publicly complaining about the mistreatment of black people on the city buses. At the beginning of the Montgomery Bus Boycott, she wrote to the paper to express her support for Rosa Parks and the protestors. She said that people should "be moved with admiration at the quiet dignity, discipline and dedication with which the Negroes have conducted their boycott."

As a result, she was shunned by the white community and

received multiple death threats. The mayor demanded that the library fire her. They didn't, but they did ask that she not write any more letters. White patrons were tearing up their library cards because of what they saw as her public betrayal. To protect the library, she stopped writing letters about the buses but continued to advocate for an end to segregation.

The central library in Montgomery is now named in honor of Juliette Hampton Morgan for her role as an early ally in the Civil Rights Movement.

Discussion Question: Why do you think Juliette Hampton Morgan has been left out of most books and movies about the Montgomery Bus Boycott?

6

The Flood

Despite all of the victories– large and small– of the 1940s and 1950s, travel in the south could still be very dangerous for black people. A New York City mailman named Victor Hugo Green created the Negro Motorist Green Book. If you were going on a road trip in your car, the Green Book showed you all the safe places to eat, get gas, 

Public Domain Image

sleep, and even find entertainment along the way. The book was published from 1936 to 1967.

But what about the people who relied on buses for long trips? There was no guide for them, except their lifelong knowledge of segregation. They knew the southern states were hanging on to their way of life, even though the courts had ruled against them.

The CORE Freedom Riders(Again)

James Farmer
Public Domain Image

By 1961, James Farmer was president of the Congress of Racial Equality (CORE), the group that carried out the 1947 Journey of Reconciliation. Again, Civil Rights leaders warned them that it was too dangerous to take integrated bus rides to the south. But again CORE was determined to demonstrate that southern states were violating the Supreme Court's decision.

The Freedom Rides were the second chapter of the Journey of Reconciliation. They planned to follow some of the same tactics as before: travel in pairs– one black, one white– and start the journey in Washington D.C., and divide themselves between Greyhound and Trailways buses. But this time they were going through the deep south. They planned a two-week trip that would end in New Orleans on the anniversary of the historic *Brown v. Board of Education* decision, where they would celebrate their success.

CORE members attended nonviolence training in Washington DC. They knew that violence was likely. But they also knew that remaining nonviolent themselves, it would make their attackers seem more ridiculous. Nobody wanted violence, but if it came, it would bring more attention to their cause.

They set out on May 4, 1961. Freedom Rider Jerry Moore

recalled, " The first day getting on the bus, it was a good feeling…we were together. It was a good cause. We were going for the movement. We were going for the people." Civil rights leader John Lewis remembered feeling like "a soldier in a nonviolent army." He would later become famous as the first person to cross the Edmund Pettis Bridge in Selma, on what is now known as Bloody Sunday.

The first few days were peaceful…

When the buses arrived in Atlanta, they had the pleasure of meeting Dr. Martin Luther King, Jr. He was living there and co-pastoring his father's church, Ebenezer Baptist. They hoped he would join them on the ride. Instead, he warned them that there would surely be violence in Alabama. King had been told by friends that the KKK planned to attack the riders. Not only was he not going with them, he wished they wouldn't go either.

To make matters worse, James Farmer's father passed away on the same day the group received Dr. King's warning. He, their leader, had to leave the Freedom Riders just as they were reaching the most dangerous part of their trip.

May 14th was Mother's Day, a beautiful warm Sunday morning boasting a clear, blue sky. The two buses carrying Freedom Riders left Atlanta heading to Birmingham. When the Greyhound bus reached the Anniston, Alabama station, 63 miles outside of Birmingham, over a hundred men surrounded the bus and slashed its tires. They shouted death threats at the Freedom Riders.

The bus driver tried to drive away but the flattened tires brought the bus to a stop.

The people on the bus, Freedom Riders and innocent passengers who just happened to be traveling that day, were terrified. Someone in the mob used a crowbar to break out the back windows. The next thing they knew, a firebomb was hurling in.

The mob ran away, knowing the bus was about to explode. That gave the passengers time to get out just before the blast.

As the passengers came off, many bleeding from shattered glass and gasping from smoke inhalation, some in the crowd tried to help them. Others attacked. Finally, a highway patrolman fired a shot in the air to break up the crowd.

Source: Birmingham Civil Rights Museum

Those on the Trailways bus were also met with extreme violence. As the bus approached the Birmingham bus station, a mob formed, many of them carrying pipes, sticks, and baseball bats. They climbed onto the bus and beat the riders for almost 10 minutes before the police arrived. Nine people were badly injured. Luckily, no one was killed.

Reports and images of the two attacks spread across America and were shown on the news in other countries. The hatred and brutality in Alabama were on display to the entire world. National leaders who had tried to ignore the Civil Rights Movement were now forced to react. The president, John F. Kennedy, called for an end to the Freedom Rides.

The following day, the injured Riders were released from the hospital. One of them was James Peck. He had been active in many social movements since the 1930s and was arrested with Bayard Rustin during the Journey of Reconciliation in 1947. He'd been beaten on the Trailways bus and had over 50 stitches. With bandages covering much of his head and face, he insisted that the rides must go on. In an interview, he declared, "We must not surrender to violence."

They gathered at the bus station in Birmingham, planning to finish the journey. They had to walk through a growing crowd to enter the station. Tension was thick. Some of these people had come to harm them, others to see what would happen next. The bus driver feared more violence, and he refused to drive the bus with the Freedom Riders on it. With no one willing to drive them and many of them badly beaten, they decided that they had gone as far as they could go. The CORE members decided their Freedom Rides were over.

They would fly to New Orleans, instead. But there was another mob waiting for them at the airport. Someone threatened to bomb the plane. The riders were stranded in the airport for several hours, unsure of their next move.

When the president sent one of his assistants, John Seigen-thaler, to help, the airlines got them on a flight as quickly as they could. Many of the Freedom Riders had never been on an airplane before.

When they arrived in New Orleans, there was a line of state police there to protect them as they got off the plane. People yelled hateful, racist remarks at the riders as they passed. Everyone thought the Freedom Rides were over.

Enter Diane Nash.

Source: The Tennessean

The SNCC Freedom Riders

Just past her teen years, Diane Nash was already a seasoned activist. In 1960, she became one of the founders of the Student Nonviolent Coordinating Committee (SNCC) after she and three other Fisk University students successfully desegregated Nashville's lunch counters. In May 1961, she was fresh off of a jail sentence in South Carolina for violating segregation laws there. Nash would later go on to work with the Southern Christian Leadership Conference on several civil rights **campaigns**.

When the CORE Freedom Riders called it quits, Nash and SNCC stepped in to finish the rides.

> It was clear to me that if we allowed the freedom rides to stop at that point, just after so much violence...the message would have been sent that all you have to do to stop a nonviolent campaign is to inflict massive violence. It was critical that the freedom ride not stop. And that we continue immediately.

All of the SNCC members were college students. They dropped out of school in the middle of their final exams to travel to Alabama and finish what CORE had started. Some of them were the first in their families to go to college, and their parents were spending hard-earned money to pay for their education. Throwing away a whole semester was not an easy choice. There were 10 in the original group, 7 men and 3 women. Eight others committed to finishing the ride if these 10 were killed or injured too badly to continue. Diane Nash would lead them.

They knew there was more violence to come. As a white SNCC member, Jim Zwerg knew he would be a target:

> As a white person, I was the primary focus of most of the violence that took place, because I was a disgrace to the white race. I was the traitor. So I knew that if anybody was probably gonna get pretty well beaten or killed, it would be me.

Before leaving Nashville, each of them wrote a **will** and a letter to their family in case they didn't make it back.

They arrived in Birmingham on May 17th. Police Chief Bull Connor, a die-hard segregationist, arrested them as soon as they arrived at the bus station.

In the middle of the night, they were taken out of jail and driven to the state line where Alabama meets Tennessee. The police cars pulled over, made the Freedom Riders get out on the side of the road, threw their luggage onto the ground, and drove away. The riders didn't know what to do. Were they being followed or watched? They didn't even know exactly where they were, but they knew they weren't safe.

They found an old, ragged-looking house and knocked on

the door. An old black man answered and swiftly told them they couldn't stay there. They decided to talk loud enough to wake up his wife, thinking she might be more helpful. Their plan worked, and the old woman allowed the 10 young activists to stay in their home overnight.

The next day, they made their way back to Birmingham. By that time, another group of students had arrived from Nashville to join them.

They all ended up stranded again, this time in the Birmingham bus station. The bus drivers refused to drive any bus they boarded. So they protested segregation by sitting in the 'White Only' waiting room.

A mob of hundreds formed outside the station. Some local men came inside to step on their feet and throw cold water in their faces.

In the meantime, President Kennedy was demanding that Alabama law enforcement protect the riders. He did not want more violence that would embarrass America in the eyes of the world. Kennedy threatened to send in the military if Alabama couldn't get the situation under control. The governor assured him that the freedom riders would be protected and would make it to Montgomery safely.

On May 20, state troopers surrounded the bus, with a helicopter overhead for added security. They escorted the riders to the Montgomery city limits, and then they left. The riders assumed that the Montgomery police department would take over providing protection.

But when the bus pulled into the Montgomery bus station, they were on their own except for a group of news reporters waiting to capture their arrival.

A growing mob attacked the reporters first. They wanted them to leave so they couldn't record what was about to happen. As the bus approached the station, the mob surrounded it. People had baseball bats, chains, and homemade weapons of every kind.

Jim Zwerg was the first one off the bus. He was beaten and stomped until he blacked out. John Lewis was hit in the head with a wooden crate. The female students were punched in the face and kicked by men in the crowd, while women stood by shouting "Kill them n*ggers!" Seigenthaler, the president's assistant, was beaten as he tried to help a female Freedom Rider escape. Reports say the mob was at least 300 people, maybe as many as 1000. Montgomery police looked on as they continued to beat the riders for several minutes. When the "Montgomery Riot" was finally stopped by police tear gas, over 20 people were badly injured.

The president decided to send in the US Marshals.

Civil rights leaders knew they, too, had to respond. They called for a mass meeting at First Baptist Church in Montgomery where Ralph Abernathy was the pastor. Abernathy was a good friend of Dr. King's and had been a key figure in the bus boycott. Reverend Fred Shuttlesworth came from Birmingham, C.T. Vivian from Nashville. Other than Vivian, these men had not supported the Freedom Rides at first. Now they wanted to make it clear that they stood with the young activists. The violence in Montgomery could not go unanswered.

On the evening of May 21st, 1500 people filled First Baptist Church. They wanted to see the civil rights leaders and the brave college students who had put themselves in harm's way.

A mob surrounded the church and began throwing rocks at the windows. The people inside were trapped. They saw a fire start outside and feared the church would be firebombed. President Kennedy called for the Marshalls to go and protect the church. Mail carriers and other federal workers were **deputized** to increase their numbers. Most of them arrived at the church in mail trucks. They tried using tear gas on the crowd outside. But the wind blew it back in their faces.

Martin Luther King called the president's brother, Attorney General Bobby Kennedy, from inside the church. Kennedy pressured Alabama's governor to put the city under **martial law**. This is when the U.S. military takes over the role of local law enforcement.

The people in the church celebrated. The President of the United States had taken their side, and help was on the way.

Soon, 700 national guardsmen filled the streets of Montgomery to prevent any more mob violence. The Freedom Riders went into hiding to avoid being arrested for violating segregation laws. None of the people who beat them were ever charged with any crimes, despite the fact that much of the riot was captured in pictures and on video.

Hidden in the home of a local activist, they again asked Dr. King to join them once they were able to safely leave Alabama. Again, he refused.

President Kennedy was determined to get the Freedom Riders out of Alabama. On Monday, May 24, 120 National guardsmen protected them as they departed on a 7 a.m. bus headed to Jackson, Mississippi, the last major city before New Orleans. This was day 21 of what was supposed to be a 14-day journey.

Even though both sets of Freedom Riders– CORE and SNCC– had been met with extreme violence in Alabama, they expected Mississippi to be worse. Throughout the Civil Rights Movement, it had been the most violent place in America. A Freedom Rider named Bernard Lafayett said, "In spite of all that Alabama had done, the fear of Mississippi, in the minds of many, was far greater."

But when the bus approached the station in Jackson, the surrounding street was quiet and virtually empty. The governor of Mississippi had requested that people stay home. Mississippi law enforcement would handle the "outside agitators."

Parchman

They exited the bus in Jackson, confused by the absence of a violent mob, and entered the station. No one bothered them. When they gathered in the 'Whites Only' waiting room, an officer told them to move along. They remained. He told them two more times. When they didn't move, he placed them under arrest. There was a **paddy wagon** waiting outside to take them to jail.

The state of Mississippi had made a deal with President Kennedy. If they would keep the Freedom Riders safe, they could arrest them for "breach of peace" and put them in prison rather than holding them in the city jail. That should teach them a lesson.

The Freedom Riders were hurried into court, found guilty, and sent to the Parchman prison farm, the most feared prison in the south. Freedom Rider David Fankhauser described the conditions there.

> In our cells, we were given a Bible, an aluminum cup, and a toothbrush. The cell measured 6 × 8 feet with a toilet and sink on the back wall and a bunk bed. We were permitted one shower per week, and no mail was allowed. The policy in the maximum security block was to keep lights on 24 hours a day...Breakfast every morning was black coffee strongly flavored with chicory, grits, biscuits, and blackstrap molasses. Lunch was generally some form of beans or black-eyed peas boiled with pork gristle, served with cornbread. In the evening, it was the same as lunch except it was cold.

Mississippi was trying to beat them at their own game. No violence. Mississippi wanted to break their spirits, to get them to give up.

Parchman became the new focus of the Freedom Rides. They decided they would fill up the prison. More riders would come and keep coming until the state of Mississippi couldn't hold them all.

College students from across the country volunteered to become Freedom Riders. They rode buses to Jackson

Mississippi, black and white together. As soon as they arrived at the bus station, they were hurried into court and sentenced to Parchman. Religious leaders came too, from many denominations. They too were arrested, quickly put on trial, and sent to Parchman.

Soon, there were over 200 Freedom Riders there. They sang freedom songs to taunt the guards. When the guards threatened to take away their mattresses, they still sang. When they threatened to take away their toothbrushes, the Freedom Riders learned to sing through tight lips.

Attorney General Bobby Kennedy pressured movement leaders to stop the Freedom Rides, to let the federal government apply pressure on the southern states to outlaw segregation. But the Supreme Court had spoken years earlier and had been ignored. So instead, movement leaders applied their own pressure to Mississippi. Freedom Riders flooded into Jackson– now they came on trains as well– until their number swelled to over 430. Three hundred of them were in Parchman.

The most violent prison in the most violent state in America was now being called a University of Nonviolence. Freedom Riders had come from different parts of the country, they were of different races, ages, and religions. But they were unified in their determination to put an end to segregation on public transportation.

Mississippi had taken its best shot. And the Freedom Riders had fought back by using its best weapon– prison– to their own advantage.

This had been a different kind of protest. Delores Boyd

lived in Montgomery and was one of the people trapped in that church on the night after the "Montgomery Riot."

> "The freedom riders introduced the notion that there were fair-minded white persons who were willing to sacrifice themselves, their bodies and their lives, because they too believed that the country had an obligation to uphold its constitutional mandate of liberty and justice for all. And I think it opened our eyes so that we didn't paint all white people with the same broad brush."

The key role of white allies would show up in every future movement, especially the voting rights struggle, commonly remembered for the Selma to Montgomery marches.

On September 22, 1961, the Interstate Commerce Commission ordered that all 'White Only' and 'Colored Only' signs must be removed from public transit facilities. In order for the bus and train companies to continue to operate in the United States, all forms of segregation– including separate seating– had to end. The battle to integrate public transportation was officially over.

Court Cases. Boycotts. Beatings. Bombings. Singing. Speeches. Soldiers. Hundreds of arrests. It took all of these. And the commitment not to give up until the battle was won. This victory fueled many others. Leaders in the public transportation struggle– Dr. King, Rosa Parks, Aurelia Browder, Jo Ann Robinson, Thurgood Marshall, C.T. Vivian, John Lewis, Diane Nash, Jim Zwerg, and others– also showed up as leaders in the fight for voting rights and to bring an end to segregation in jobs and housing.

In a speech following the ICC ruling, President Kennedy foreshadowed what was to come. "A great change is at hand, and our task, our obligation is to make that revolution, that change, peaceful and **constructive** for all."

Less than two years later, he proposed a Civil Rights Act ending all segregation in the United States. It was passed into law on July 2, 1964, seven months after his assassination.

campaign- the push to achieve a specific goal

will- directions for what to do with a person's belongings after they die

deputized- named a law enforcement officer

martial law- a temporary military takeover of government and law enforcement

paddy wagon- a police van with a mobile cell inside

constructive- useful, helpful

Chapter 6 Discussion Questions

1. The Freedom Riders wanted to demonstrate that southern states were still segregating people, even though this was illegal. Why was it important to put this on display?

2. Why did the CORE Freedom Riders want to end their trip on the anniversary of the *Brown* decision?

3. Diane Nash played an important role in many civil rights campaigns, but few people have ever heard of her. Why do you think this is?

4. Why would protestors use violence to try to prevent black- and white people from riding together on buses?

5. Why do you think the guards at Parchman punished Freedom Riders for singing?

6. Is it okay to get arrested if you're fighting for a good cause? Explain your response.

Public Domain Image

References

Arsenault, Raymond (2006). *Freedom Riders: 1961 and the Struggle for Racial Justice.* Oxford University Press.

Beito, David T.; Beito, Linda Royster (2009). *Black Maverick: T.R.M. Howard's Fight for Civil Rights and Economic Power.* Urbana: University of Illinois Press.

Blair L. M. Kelley (2010). *Right to Ride: Streetcar Boycotts and African American Citizenship in the Era of Plessy v. Ferguson.* John Hope Franklin Series in African American History and Culture.

Borger, Julian (April 3, 2006). "Civil rights heroes may get pardons". *The Guardian.*

Carawan, Guy; Carawan, Candie, eds. (2008). "1961: Freedom Rides". *Sing for Freedom: The Story of the Civil Rights Movement Through Its Songs.* NewSouth Books.

Cockrell, D. (1997). *Demons of disorder: Early blackface minstrels and their world.* Cambridge: Cambridge University Press.

DC Historic Preservation Office (n.d.), "Civil Rights Tour: Employment - Elmer Henderson, Fighter for Equality," *DC Historic Sites.*

D'Emilio, John (2004). *Lost Prophet: The Life and Times of Bayard Rustin.* Chicago: The University of Chicago Press.

Elaine Elinson (January 16, 2012), San Francisco's own Rosa Parks, *San Francisco Chronicle.*

Frazier, Nishani (2017). *Harambee City: Congress of Racial Equality in Cleveland and the Rise of Black Power Populism.*

Garrow, David J. (1989). *The Walking City.* Brooklyn, NY: Carlson Publishing Inc.

Goldstein, Richard (August 13, 2007). "Irene Morgan Kirkaldy, 90, Rights Pioneer, Dies". *The New York Times.*

Greider, Katherine (November 13, 2005). "The Schoolteacher on the Streetcar". *New York Times.*

Haskins, James (1997). *Bayard Rustin: Behind the Scenes of the Civil Rights Movement* (New York: Hyperion.

Hearth, Amy Hill (2018). *Streetcar to Justice: How Elizabeth Jennings Won the Right to Ride in New York.* Harper Collins/Greenwillow Books.

Hoose, Phillip M. (2009). *Claudette Colvin: Twice toward Justice.* New York: Melanie Kroupa Books/Farrar Straus Giroux.

Hudson, Lynn Marie (2003). *The Making of "Mammy Pleasant": A Black Entrepreneur in Nineteenth-century.* University of Illinois Press.

Jakoubek, Robert (1989). *Martin Luther King, Jr. Civil Rights Leader.* Philadelphia: Chelsea House Publishers.

Johnson II, Lucas L. (18 May 2007). "South moving to pardon disobedience convictions". Associated Press.

Lipsitz, George (2011). *How racism takes place.* Philadelphia: Temple University Press.

Matteson, Noelle (2011). *The Freedom Rides and Alabama: A Guide to Key Events and Places, Context, and Impact.* New South Books.

McCabe, Katie; Roundtree, Dovey Johnson (2009). *Justice Older Than the Law: The Life of Dovey Johnson Roundtree.* University Press of Mississippi.

McCloskey, Robert G. & Levinson, Sanford (2010). *The American Supreme Court (5th ed.).* Chicago: University of Chicago Press.

McGuire, Danielle (2010). *At the Dark End of the Stree.* New York: Alfred A. Knopf.

McGrew, Jannell (December 4, 2018). "Aurelia Shines Browder Coleman, Lead plaintiff in the Supreme Court case, helped quash public transit segregation. *Montgomery Advertiser.*

Meier, August & Rudwick, Elliott (1969). "The First Freedom Ride". *Phylon.* 30 (3): 213–222

Morello, Carol (July 30, 2000). "The Freedom Rider a Nation Nearly Forgot: Woman Who Defied Segregation Finally Gets Her Due." *Washington Post.*

Nelson, S. (Director, Writer). (2011). *Freedom riders.* [Film] American Experience Films, WGBH Educational Foundation: PBS Distribution.

Newman, Janet, Yates, Nicola, et al (2008). *Social Justice.* Open University Press.

Smith, Bonnie G., ed. (2008). "The Oxford Encyclopedia of Women in World History, Volume 1". Oxford University Press.

Shay, Alison (November 7, 2012). University of North Carolina at Chapel Hill "Remembering Sarah Keys."

Thamel, Pete (January 1, 2006). "Grier Integrated a Game and Earned the World's Respect". *New York Times*.

Thornton, J. Mills (2006). *Dividing Lines: Municipal Politics and the Struggle for Civil Rights in Montgomery, Birmingham, and Selma.* University of Alabama Press.

Toll, R. C. (1974). *Blacking up: The minstrel show in nineteenth-century America.* New York, NY: Oxford University Press.

Walker, Robert J. (2007). *Let My People Go!: The Miracle of the Montgomery Bus Boycott.* Lanham, MD: Hamilton Books.

Wright, Barnett (April 19, 2018). "What's inside Montgomery's national peace and slave memorial museum opening April 26."

Zellner, Bob (2011). *The Wrong Side of Murder Creek: A White Southerner in the Freedom Movement.* NewSouth Books.

About the Author

 Simone Ray Thomas is a native of Denver, CO. She is an alumna of Tuskegee University and received a doctorate in Education from the University of Memphis. She has two children- Amani Simone and Daryl Ramon, Jr.- and one granddaughter, Aniya Simone. She has worked in Education since 1997 and currently lives in Alabama.

Simone's "Tuskegee Lake Poem", was published in the *Agnieska's Dowry* collection in 1997. She has since edited a range of projects and written for local publications in Chicago and Memphis.

The UNHEARD OF imprint was created to illuminate the often-overlooked historic contributions of black Americans. Other UNHEARD OF books include *365 Days of Black Men in History* (2016) and *Father of the Movement: Vernon Johns* (2022).

Contact unheardbooks@gmail.com for more information.